This is a 'sixty minute' book, so it can be read in an hour (in a bit of a rush!). If you don't have time to read it all, every so often there are sixty second pages that sum up what's gone before – and if you don't even have time for them, there are two one second pages that sum up the whole book!

To my husband Paul – you're brilliant!
And also to Millie, a great pal.

THE
Sixty
MINUTE
DEBT BUSTER

An hour to transform your finances

Katie Clarke
with Rob Parsons

LION

A Lion Book
an imprint of
Lion Hudson plc
Wilkinson House, Jordan Hill Road,
Oxford OX2 8DR, England

www.lionhudson.com

ISBN 978 0 7459 5342 7 (UK)

Distributed by:
UK: Marston Book Services, PO Box 269, Abingdon, Oxon, OX14
4YN
USA: Trafalgar Square Publishing, 814 N. Franklin Street,
Chicago, IL 60610
USA: Christian Market: Kregel Publications, PO Box 2607, Grand
Rapids, Michigan 49501

First edition 2009
10 9 8 7 6 5 4 3 2 1 0

Acknowledgments
Katie Clarke would like to thank Jonathan Booth, Jonathan
Mason, Sheron Rice, Lynda Reid and Andrew Buchanan-Smith.
Special thanks to agent Eddie Bell of the Bell Lomax Moreton
Agency, Lomax Moreton Agency, editor Kate Kirkpatrick and all
the team at Lion Hudson.

This book has been printed on paper and board independently
certified as having been produced from sustainable forests.

A catalogue record for this book is availablefrom the British
Library

Typeset in ITS Stone Serif 10.5/15

Printed and bound in Great Britain by CPI Cox & Wyman,
Reading.

Contents

Chapter 1

You've Come to the Right Place

Life at the debt counselling centre was never ordinary. It was a fascinating place located in an old terraced house. You could say it was a bit rough round the edges – the decoration left a lot to be desired and the roof was leaking – and it was certainly a far cry from my previous office, a swanky pad near the Royal Courts of Justice in London. My office was so small that if a client brought a couple of family members to their appointment for moral support, it reminded me of those challenges to see how many people you can fit into a telephone box! And yet, this place did an incredible job in the local community. All sorts of people from all walks of life would step through the big old blue door every day. This centre was so popular that the appointment diary was regularly booked up several weeks in advance. Many clients said that despite their problems the place felt like a safe haven, a sanctuary.

In the job, it was impossible to predict what a day would hold. As I helped people to get out of debt, I listened to their stories, negotiated with banks, credit card companies and loan sharks on their behalf and provided an endless supply of tissues and cups of tea. When things got really desperate and it looked as though someone was going to lose their home, I would get on my feet in court and fight their corner.

I remember one day in particular. It was a Monday morning. I had a headache and had just knocked back a couple of aspirin. I was hoping for a quiet day when the internal phone rang. Sally, our receptionist, was one of the calmest women I have ever known. She had to be. When clients walked into our advice centre for the first time they were almost always emotional. Sally has comforted some people, befriended others and threatened to call the police more than once. But I could tell from the tone of her voice that even she was rattled: 'Katie, can you pop out as soon as possible?' she whispered down the phone. 'There's a man out here who says that he won't leave until he sees someone.'

I took a few deep breaths and went out to the front office. I'm not sure what I was expecting to see, but there he was: an elderly man sat in the corner of the waiting area, not making eye contact with anyone and gently sobbing. I grabbed the box of tissues from Sally's desk and sat myself down next to him. 'I'm Katie,' I said, 'and you must be Mr Davidson.' I helped him up and led him into my office.

As he sat down he said, 'I'm sorry, love. I don't know

what's got into me.'

'Please don't worry now. I'm here to help you. What can I do for you?'

He didn't reply, just bent down and lifted a well-worn shopping bag onto my desk. I pulled it towards me and peeked in. And then I knew at once what it was. I have seen it many times – in Sainsbury's carriers, in black rubbish sacks and holdalls. This was the debt bag.

I upended it and the contents spilled over my desk and onto the floor. There were letters from credit card companies, banks, gas and electricity companies and debt collection agencies. Almost every one of them bore some kind of threat. On the oldest letters the threats, though frightening, were less intimidating: 'Your overdraft may be recalled', 'Your credit rating may be affected', 'Your account may be terminated'. But then on the most recent ones the threats were brazen and terrifying: 'Bailiffs will seize your goods', 'You will have to appear in court', 'You may be made bankrupt and lose your home'.

It was this last letter that had finally brought Adam Davidson into my advice centre.

'I know you'll think I'm stupid, love,' he began, 'but it was the credit cards that did it. I'd never had one until five years ago, but they kept writing to me and I thought it'd be nice to give the wife a holiday and put the new kitchen in. And I know it sounds silly, but after that I just don't know what happened. I found it hard to make the payments and then I took out another card and used it to pay the first one off. And then I did the same with another one. And even then, they kept offering me more.'

I rummaged amongst the papers until I found a credit card statement. I read it for a moment and then said, 'Do you know what rate of interest you are being charged on this card?'

He shook his head. 'I never read the small print, love. Aren't they all the same?'

When I told him that it was just above 30%, he shook his head and said, 'I don't understand it all.'

And then he started to cry again. 'The worst part is that the wife doesn't know. How am I going to tell her we're going to lose the bungalow?'

I reassured him that there was a lot that could be done to save his home. We would work through everything together and hopefully be able to reach an agreement with everyone to whom he owed money. I asked him how much was left on his mortgage. He said, 'Nothing. We paid it off years ago with the money they gave me when I left the army.'

I quickly sorted the demands and bills into piles. 'Are you sure there's nothing else?' I asked. He nodded.

'So you've got £25,000 of credit card debt, you owe the gas company £180, the telephone company £80 and the electric people £200?'

He looked totally ashamed. 'Yes, love. It's the credit cards that are the big ones.'

'Well, Adam,' I said, 'I want you to try as best you can to stop worrying. Yes, you have got a lot of debt, but one way or another, we'll get through this together. This is what I want you to do. First, I want you to tell your wife that you've been to see me and make an appointment for you both to come in. I know you're only trying to protect her, but it's important that you share this with her so you can support each other in getting through this. Adam, I can't make you any promises but I will help you fight to keep your home.'

And then something amazing happened. I had a glimpse of the Adam Davidson before debt took over his life. A huge smile stretched across his face and he said, 'If you can do that, you'll have saved my life.' And when he smiled I knew why I was stuck in a seven foot by ten foot office with a computer that made the old Commodore 64 look state-of-the-art and a door that stuck in the winter.

Debt is a killer. It makes you feel stupid, ashamed, trapped. But I can tell you this – all kinds of people have crossed the threshold of my little office: people on benefits and those on large incomes, people who are in danger of being evicted from their council homes and those with large property portfolios, the unemployed and, on one occasion, a financial advisor. Debt doesn't pick and choose.

It may be that you're not in a lot of debt and you just want to handle your money more effectively. This book will help you. But perhaps either you or somebody you care about is in deep financial trouble. If that's the case, you're reading the right book.

I have no doubt that somebody will be reading right now who is beside themselves with worry about money – and their head is spinning. If that's you, take a breath and at least take on board what I am about to say next:

The problem with worry over debt is that it *isolates*

you. You will often be afraid to tell your partner, your friends or relatives – or even to get some help from professionals. But you *can* come through this experience. Tens of thousands of people have been in your situation and have done just that. It may be that none of this is your fault or perhaps you have been foolish with money. But whatever the reason, it won't change the fact that none of us can do anything about yesterday. Today you are going to start the process of getting out of debt.

So let's begin.

Quiz

It's a frightening statistic that people in the UK spend almost twice as long planning for a holiday as arranging a mortgage.[1] But what about you? Just how financially in control are you?

Have a look at the following questions and answer each one as honestly as possible. At the end you will get points depending on your responses. I'm not saying this is the most accurate barometer of financial health ever devised by man – so don't worry too much about the results – but it does give you an idea of the kind of issues you should be thinking about if you want to take a firm grip on your finances.

1. Do you always pay your credit cards off in full each month? *Always/sometimes/never*

2. Do you know how much interest you are paying on your credit cards? *Always/sometimes/never*

3. Do you know how much money you have in your current account? *Always/sometimes/never*

4. When you want to make a fairly major purchase or take out insurance etc., do you shop around to find the best deal? *Always/sometimes/never*

5. When you want to buy something, do you save up for it? *Always/sometimes/never*

6. Do you put aside some money into savings each month? *Always/sometimes/never*

7. Can you quickly put your hands on important financial paperwork such as credit card bills, mortgage documents etc.?
Always/sometimes/never

8. Do you go shopping as a 'pick me up', regardless of whether you can afford it?
Always/sometimes/never

9. Do you regularly rely on your overdraft?
Always/sometimes/never

10. Do you use your credit card to pay for everyday expenses, like food and petrol?
Always/sometimes/never

Now for your scores! For questions 1–7, give yourself 2 points for every 'Always', 1 point for every 'Sometimes' and 0 points for every 'Never'. For questions 8–10, it's 0 points for 'Always', 1 point for 'Sometimes' and 2 points for 'Never'.

15 to 20: Well done! You seem to really have your wits about you where your finances are concerned. But do make sure you are getting some enjoyment out of your money as well – it's easy to get so consumed by saving for that rainy day that you never buy a pair of sunglasses!

10 to 14: You seem to be quite well balanced in your approach to money. You really want to make your money work for you both for today and in the future. Just make sure you keep a regular check on yourself and that the balance doesn't start to tip into the red!

5 to 9: You have got some of the right ideas but no doubt you often feel out of control. Spend some time organizing yourself. Put into practice some of the tips in this book – they will make a big difference to you.

0 to 4: You seem to be a bit reckless in your approach to your money but maybe you haven't always been like this. You need to take action before this situation spirals further out of control. Seek the support of a friend or family member, or you may feel that it's got to the stage where some professional advice would be welcome. If so, make an appointment at your local advice centre today. And keep reading!

Look after the pennies...

• Collect loyalty points and check out the best way to get value for money with them. However, don't be persuaded to buy a more expensive product just to get the loyalty points – always shop in the cheapest place.

• Plan ahead when booking train tickets – there are usually cheaper tickets available if you get them early enough.

• Consider buying an annual discount card for train travel. Check out www.railcard.co.uk to get more information.

• Make use of offers for the cinema and theatre. Many cinemas have a cheaper night, and there's also Orange Wednesdays, through which Orange mobile customers can get 2 for 1 tickets. For theatre, www.lastminute.com and many theatres have last-minute half-price tickets.

• Keep on top of car maintenance – this will ensure that your car's petrol consumption is more efficient.

• Don't carry big items in your car, such as prams, roof-racks or golf clubs, unless you need them that day – a heavier load will increase petrol consumption.

• Don't wait until your petrol tank is empty before filling it up – you're less likely to find a cheaper petrol station that way.

• Join your local library rather than buying books you only read once.

• Give up the daily visit to the coffee shop – it's amazing just how much this adds up to over a year.

• If you possibly can, give up smoking. Go on. You know you should!

Chapter 2

Sizing Up the Problem

So you've made the decision that you need to take action. You're going into battle against your debt. This is a real turning point. But first you need to see what you're up against. It's likely to be painful, but we need to know how strong the opposition is and what resources you've got to fight with. So how big is the enemy? How much debt are you actually in?

To answer those questions, I'm now going to send you on a mission. Prepare yourself, it may be tough! The task is for you to scour your home for your latest bank statements, credit card bills and letters from anybody to whom you owe money (your creditors). If you are organized, you will go straight to the place where these are filed alphabetically and according to creditor and date. 'Yeah, fat chance!' I hear you thinking. OK, so maybe you are more like the majority of people and accomplishing the mission will involve rummaging in your bedside cabinet, under the coffee table in the lounge, on the kitchen worktop... oh, and not forgetting the top of the fridge and behind the sofa!

Ten hours later...

Finally, this part of the mission is complete. You've done your best to gather all the bits of paper that tell how much you owe. Now take the papers and put them in piles according to each debt, placing the latest letter for each debt on the top of its pile. Next, make a list of each debt and how much is owed. OK, so now we know the size of the enemy army, but how ugly are they? Let's find out. Note down any rates of interest that you are being charged so that you can see which debts are costing you the most.

Below is an example of how this might look. (There's a blank version of this table at the back of the book for you to use.)

Debt	Amount owed	Interest rate (%)
Gas	£72	
Electricity	£53	
Mortgage	£635	
Council tax	£369	
Hire purchase on car	£3,750	6.90%
Bank overdraft	£187	18.80%
Bank loan	£1,645	6.90%
Credit card 1	£250	17.00%
Credit card 2	£820	19.00%
Credit card 3	£810	19.00%
Store card	£120	29.90%
Catalogue purchases	£100	29.80%
TOTAL	**£8,811**	

So now you know the worst. It may be quite scary to see the true situation in black and white and maybe you owe a lot more than you thought. But there *are* solutions and you can bet your bottom dollar (actually, perhaps not a good idea) that there are people out there who had a far more frightening list than you and who have cleared their debts. You have taken the first step, which is always the hardest.

Get ready for the second part of the war against debt: you have to work out what weapons you have for the fight. There are normally three you will need in order to win this war – Money, Willpower and Support – or Dosh, Discipline and... Dead Good Help (that's this book, by the way!) It's now time for you to take a health check on your monthly finances, and for this, you are going to make a list of your income and expenditure and create your own personal budget. It's going to take a bit of time, so put the kettle on and get the biscuits ready. If you have a partner, it might be a good idea to sit down and work through this together.

First, the easier part of the task: note down each element of your income. This means every single source of money that you have coming in, whether it's salary, benefits, interest on savings, maintenance, rental income... you get the idea. If you are having problems, it may help to refer to your bank statement or building society account book. Your list of income might look like this:

Income	£/month
Wages	£607.26
Partner's wages	
Overtime	
Partner's overtime	
Bonuses	
Partner's bonuses	
Pension	
Child benefit	£72.40
Income support	
Jobseeker's Allowance	
Tax credits	£434.00
Maintenance/child support	
Interest on savings	
Other income (1)	
(2)	
(3)	
(4)	
TOTAL	**£1,113.66**

Now for the harder bit – itemize everything that you spend your money on. Remember to be consistent and use monthly *or* weekly figures throughout. Many people say that they just don't know where their money goes each month. Most of us have been in the situation where the tenner we withdraw from the cash point is gone before we know it and without us really knowing where it went. If you can identify with this, then this should be an enlightening exercise. Some things are easy to remember – all the regular bills such as mortgage/rent, council tax, gas, electricity and such like – but then you've got the other things you spend your money on: food, clothes, cinema, sandwiches, coffees, gym membership, magazines. It can be frightening when you realize just how long the list is and how much they all add up. Have your bank statements to hand when you're doing this and you can check them through to ensure that you include all the direct debits and standing orders which are set up on your account. You will also be able to see from your statements just how many times you have been popping back and forth to the cash point.

There is a budget sheet at the back of this book which you should find really helpful with this.

Now for the moment of truth...

Compare what you've got coming in with what's going out. Aaagh!!! At least, that's what most people say. In fact, loads of people spend about 10% more than they earn. (And that goes for really high rollers as well!)

Well, so far you've used two of my 'Ds': some discipline (you found all the paperwork – OK, almost all), and you've had some dead good help (that's me!), but is there any of that third 'D' around? Because without it, we're sunk. The search is on for the dosh! And that means you have got to get that spending down so there's a little spare cash each month. Boring? Perhaps. But not as boring as never having any money for anything and being chased down the street by bailiffs.

Be ruthless and think about where you can make cutbacks. You'd be surprised. There are all sorts of places. Buying that coffee every morning on the way into work at a hit of £1.50 each day adds up to nearly £400 over the whole year. That means that if you're a basic rate taxpayer you've got to earn £580 before tax and national insurance just to pay your coffee bill! Just think how long you actually have to work to earn that! Wouldn't you rather be ploughing that money into paying off your debts? When you are eventually debt free, that kind of money could pay for a holiday.

Maybe you have a gym membership. Even as you read this, a wave of guilt is passing over you. Like so many other people, it's not the first membership you've had. Each time you start out in such earnest with rigorous exercise regimes in mind. In all fairness to you, it began well. But that was just for the first fortnight and now the gym is lucky if you grace it with your presence once a week. When you work out the amount you are actually paying per visit, it must be one of the most expensive training sessions going. Cancel it and run around the park instead! At £65 per month, that's a saving of £780 a year.

Then there are the insurances (car, house, personal) and the telephone, television and Internet packages, breakdown cover and even your mortgage (although it's much harder to swap your mortgage these days). Have you got good deals for these? By simply shopping around on the Internet, you can check whether you are paying over the odds for the services you use. By changing providers, it's often possible to make significant savings. Even if it's just £50 here and there, it's extra money in your pocket. All these cutbacks can really start to add up. For ideas on how to do this, have a look at pages 27–9.

While we're on the subject of insurance, it's staggering just how many different forms of insurance you can get these days. It seems that nearly everything is insurable from your pet gerbil to your right foot (that is, if you're David Beckham). But do we really need all of these? Consider what insurance you do need, which risks you can respond to in other ways (for example, by putting a small amount of money into your own 'insurance fund', to be used when you need it) and which risks are frankly not serious enough to warrant insurance.

You may well have Payment Protection Insurance (PPI) that you took out at the same time as a loan or credit card. It is intended to cover your payments if you fall sick, have an accident or become unemployed during the lifetime of the loan. There are a number of problems with PPI. Typically, it is incredibly expensive and as it provides significant revenue for banks, it is often given the hard sell and can be difficult to refuse. Although there is a legal obligation on the bank to check if the PPI is suitable for the person, often these checks are not carried out. Some people don't even realize they are paying for PPI because of the way that the payment for it is included in the overall borrowing figures – along with interest and other charges – for the loan.

These problems have recently hit the headlines. In fact, a major bank was fined £1.1 million by the Financial Services Authority. It was decided that they had sold PPI to customers without gathering sufficient information from them and that this resulted in the sale of policies to people who might never be able to claim under the policy.[2] The bank was one of many to be fined for their inappropriate selling of PPI.

Thousands of pounds are now being paid to people who have been missold PPI. If you think you have experienced this yourself, I would urge you to try to reclaim that money. It's worth it. It costs nothing and may only involve writing a letter to the bank. On his website, www.moneysavingexpert.com, Martin Lewis explains step by step how to go about reclaiming missold PPI.

Anyway, let's get back to that budget you're preparing. Come on, don't give up! You can make some more cutbacks. Keep going until there's some spare money each month.

And now have another go – we need to find more cash.

Now you've got something to fight with – a little extra money each month. But with all those debts, and all those people yelling to be paid, who do we give our precious dosh to first? Well, probably not those shouting loudest and certainly not those who send letters that start, 'Dear Ms Clitheroe, we regret to inform you that now you have made us really, really, really cross and if you do not send us loads of money we will put this in the hands of our solicitors.'

In fact, who you pay first is so important that we're going to dedicate a whole chapter to it...

SIXTY SECOND PAGE
SIZING UP THE PROBLEM

Gather together all statements, bills and letters to do with your debts.

Make a list of each debt and how much you owe.

Note down each part of your income.

Write down everything you spend your money on.

Ask yourself where you can make cutbacks, however small.

Look after the pennies...

• Don't automatically renew your insurance with the same provider. Compare different companies to see who offers value for money.

• When making a major purchase, shop around for the best price. I saved around £100 on my new fridge-freezer!

• Turn off the lights when you're not in a room – an average household could save £25 each year by turning out lights that are not being used.[3]

• Carry a notebook around with you for a while to note down everything that you spend your money on, however small. If you do this, you will begin to gain a true picture of where those pennies and pounds actually go. Becoming debt free requires us to be knowledgeable about our spending, actually knowing where our hard-earned money is going. Check your notebook against your bank statement.

• Prepare a budget and stick to it.

• Read the news on the Internet or watch it on television rather than buying a daily newspaper.

• If you buy a magazine regularly, take out a subscription – you will save loads.

• Turn your thermostat down by one degree and you could save 10% on your energy bills.[4]

27

• Don't go food shopping on an empty stomach – you will always spend more when you're hungry!

• Make use of 'buy one, get one free' deals.

✔ The Price is Right! (... making sure!)

When your satellite or cable package, telephone, Internet and mobile phone contracts are due for renewal, don't automatically stick with the same provider. You may be able to save yourself some money here and there by shopping around for the best deal.

• If you are thinking of switching providers, first telephone your current provider and tell them you are thinking of leaving. They don't want to lose customers and may well offer you a better deal or some incentive to stay with them.

• Then check whether you can get a cheaper deal with a different provider by using one of the price comparison websites such as www.moneysupermarket.com, www.uswitch.com or www.pricerunner.co.uk.

These websites can also be used to compare loans, credit cards, current accounts, holidays, shopping... the list goes on. By simply logging on and spending a few minutes entering some information about the product you wish to check, you could save yourself a substantial amount over the year across the range of products and services you are using. Even if you only save £50 a year, if the phone call takes you fifteen minutes that's a rate of £200 an hour – not bad, eh?

Using one of these websites, I carried out a simple comparison for buildings and contents insurance. The difference between the lowest and the highest prices quoted was over £300! And to think I might have just gone with the more expensive product had I not been able to compare right across the market.

It's not hard and it could save you money! Once you've checked if you're on the best deal, keep tabs on it – regularly shop around to ensure you are getting value for money.

Chapter 3

Who to Pay First

So you've identified how much you owe and have worked out a budget. That's a good start.

But what's the next step?

Maybe you've started to get some scary letters and phone calls from the companies to whom you owe money. They all want their money *yesterday*. It seems to make little difference when you tell them that you do have other debts; each insists that they must be paid *first*. But interestingly, it's not always those who shout the loudest who should be paid first. In fact, quite often it's the very opposite. Those companies where non-payment is most serious in the long term are often the least aggressive in their approach.

Contact your creditors and tell them that you are experiencing problems. Don't bury your head in the sand and wait for them to contact you. They prefer to be kept in the picture. This particular bull definitely needs to be grabbed by the horns; it's not going to stop chasing you because you're afraid of it.

I remember Sandra coming to see me for advice. She had pink hair, a yellow cardigan, and a string of debts – credit cards, arrears with her water bills (which had been passed on to a debt collection company), and she owed money to a couple of doorstep money lenders. These debts were causing her untold anxiety. Her creditors were telephoning her several times each day. She dreaded the post arriving and was afraid to answer her phone and even her own front door. Because of the pressure they put on her, Sandra had paid £200 to one of them just before coming to her appointment with me.

And then I noticed it. A court summons was lurking at the back of the paperwork which she had resting on her lap. I would recognize one of those anywhere! They always stick out like a sore thumb when I'm presented with a stack of letters. There's something about the logo used by Her Majesty's Court Service and the formality of the document which seems to jump out at me. When I asked Sandra about it, she said, 'Oh yes. I forgot about that one. I think it's something to do with my rent.' She was right. It was the most important document amongst that bundle. Sandra was in substantial arrears with her rent and so her landlord had issued her with court proceedings for possession of the property. She had a court date fast approaching, at which time she would need to demonstrate to the judge that she could afford to pay the rent and clear the arrears within a reasonable period of time. She would also need to show that, despite the difficult circumstances, she was trying to make an effort.

When I explained to her just how important it was for her to focus her energies on paying her rent (otherwise she would lose her home), she was adamant that she could not do this because it was the other companies who were putting on the pressure. I explained that, for the moment, little would happen to her if she did not make payments on the other debts, but she was staring eviction in the face if she didn't start to get a grip on her rent arrears. It was difficult to get the message across to Sandra. She was bombarded by calls and letters from the other companies and yet her landlord wasn't so demanding. This made it hard for her to understand that the rent should take priority.

In his book *The Money Secret*, Rob Parsons suggests a useful device to help remember which debts/bills must take priority. It's called pay THEM FIRST and each of the letters of THEM FIRST stand for one of the priority bills.

Tax (council)
Hire purchase
Electricity/gas
Maintenance and child support

Fine
Income tax
Rent/mortgage
Second mortgage
Television licence

These are often known as the 'priority debts' and when we are working out which debts/bills to pay first, it is these that must be paid before all others. This is because non-payment of these bills can have very serious implications. If we don't pay our rent or mortgage we will ultimately lose our home. If we fail to keep up with gas and electricity bills our supply can be cut off. Non-payment of maintenance, fines, income tax and the television licence can, in some circumstances, lead to imprisonment. Non-payment of council tax will ultimately result in the council obtaining a liability order and they can then instruct bailiffs, apply for your bankruptcy or get an attachment of earnings order against you – which means some of your hard-earned wages going to the council before they've even hit your bank account. And arrears on a hire purchase agreement means that the company may be able to repossess the goods (depending on the circumstances, this can sometimes be without the need for a court order). Not much fun if we need the car to get to work.

And so it's important when we are working out who gets our money first that we remember to pay THEM FIRST (even when the credit card company is calling us every day and the doorstep money lender knocks on our door every Friday). Ideally, insofar as our priority debts are concerned, this means keeping up with the normal monthly commitments and also paying them a little extra each month to reduce any arrears.

Contact the priority creditor as soon as you realize that

you will have difficulty meeting the payments and try to reach an *affordable* payment arrangement with them. It's always worth seeking free advice, as the advisor may do this for you.

If your situation is so critical that you simply cannot afford to meet the payments on the priority debts (or you cannot afford the amount the creditor is requesting), pay as much as you can afford – this will show that you are serious about clearing the debt – and seek free advice as soon as possible.

If Sandra had followed this rule of thumb then she might have avoided the experience of being taken to court and the worry of possibly losing her home.

But what about the non-priority debts?

After essential expenditure and the necessary payments to the priority creditors, your other creditors (the non-priority creditors) will want to receive a fair share of any money left over. A free legal advice centre will help you to work this out or visit www.careforthefamily.org.uk/debtbuster.

If you have no or little available income it's possible to contact the non-priority creditors and ask if they will agree to accept a payment as low as £1 per month. This is obviously only a temporary measure but gives you some breathing space to try to get things back on track. You may say, 'A pound! They'll never accept that!' Trust me, they often will. After all, it's all you can afford – and at least it's something off the arrears! Always ask for interest and charges to be frozen. (Again, I would urge you to go to a *free* debt counselling centre. They will talk to you about the amount you can realistically pay and, as with the priority debts, they may even negotiate with the creditors on your behalf.)

This is what a letter to one of your creditors might look like:

XYZ Company
25 High Road
JP23 5UF

Dear Sir/Madam
Account number : 1234 5678 9000
Your Ref : ABC DEF 123

I am currently experiencing financial difficulties.
I am married with two dependent children. I have recently had to stop working due to illness/redundancy and my wife works part-time. I enclose a copy of my budget sheet, which shows my weekly/ monthly income and expenditure.

At the moment I am unable to afford the required monthly payment on this account. I would be grateful if you would agree to accept payments of £..... for the next six months, by which time I hope that my circumstances will have improved.

I also enclose details of my other creditors and the offers that I am making to each of them. You will see that I am trying to treat all of my creditors fairly.

Finally, I would be grateful if you would agree to freeze all interest and other charges on the account.

Thank you for your help. I look forward to hearing from you.

Yours faithfully,

Charles Simpson

SIXTY SECOND PAGE
WHO TO PAY FIRST

Work out priority debts – pay THEM FIRST.

**Contact priority creditors and agree
realistic payments.
THEN**

**Pay what you can (and only what you can)
to non-priority creditors.**

Agree realistic sums with these lenders.

Request that interest be frozen.

 **DUMPING THE DEBT...**

DO obtain free legal advice – talk through the options with someone who specializes in the area and who doesn't charge for their advice. This is very important. Some companies that masquerade as debt advisors may take even more of your money. Consider going to the Citizens Advice Bureau, which can help you free of charge.

DO get organized – disorganization only makes us feel more out of control.

DO set a budget and plan your spending – this will help you to regain control.

DO reward yourself – have fun, it doesn't have to cost the earth!

DON'T go it alone – debt can be very stressful. If you have a partner, try not to keep it from them. If not, find a friend you can confide in.

DON'T bury your head in the sand – the problem won't go away.

DON'T be unrealistic in your plans to get back on track. If your budget is unachievable, you will feel demoralized.

✓ The Price is Right! (...making sure!)

• Petrol

Check out where to buy the cheapest petrol in your area by looking at www.petrolprices.com. You just have to enter your postcode and it does the rest for you. As prices of petrol are changing daily, you can even sign up to a free email alert that will tell you where to buy the cheapest petrol each day.

• Food

Food prices are constantly increasing and now thanks to websites such as www.mysupermarket.com you can work out where you will get the most value for your money. This website enables you to compare the prices of goods at Asda, Sainsbury's, Tesco and Ocado. When you get to the checkout stage, you can purchase your entire shop at the supermarket at which it would cost you the least. The website claims that its price checker scans your trolley, finding ways for you to cut your bill by up to 20% every week.

By shopping online for your groceries, you should save enough money to outweigh the delivery charge. You are more likely to stick to your shopping list when shopping on line. Buy some more basic or staple items from cheaper supermarkets such as Lidl and Aldi. Make sure you sign up to any reward schemes run by the supermarkets and you could save yourself a further 1% off your shopping bill.

The Real Cost of Credit Cards

When day broke on that Tuesday in September Carl Jenkins didn't intend to kill himself. It is true that within moments of waking his thoughts were totally consumed by his debts. He dreaded what letters demanding payment would arrive and he had only been awake a matter of minutes when the now familiar sick feeling in the pit of his stomach set in. But this was nothing new. He had felt like this every single day for the last six months – from the moment he opened his eyes in the morning until the moment he managed to get to sleep in the early hours after what seemed like a lifetime of just lying there, worrying.

Carl was in a lot of debt. In fact, he had eight credit cards on which he owed over £40,000. I wouldn't be surprised if you're wondering how on earth somebody who took home less than a thousand pounds each month from his job as a shop assistant could end up with that much debt. But unfortunately, the answer is – 'quite easily'. Carl racked up this debt during a time when banks were incredibly free with their lending. It was so easy to get a credit card, you practically just had to be able to sign your name. It was not just those with a good credit history who found it easy to borrow money. Those with poor credit ratings were also targeted, but with a catch... they were offered loans and credit cards with much higher rates of interest.

Carl fell into the second category. He started off having just one credit card with a limit of £2,000. Every month he made the minimum payment of 3% of the balance on that card. It wasn't long before the credit card company wrote to him to tell him that his credit limit had doubled. He didn't request this – they just did it. Like so many others, Carl believed that he had been offered the additional borrowing because the credit card company thought he could handle it. It didn't even cross his mind that the bank was under pressure to meet targets and to grab what they called 'market share'. In truth, he didn't really think about it, he just accepted it for what it was. He earned a handful of air miles each time he used his card and felt flattered to get the letters which told him that because he was such a 'valued customer' his credit limit was being increased.

For a while the new credit facility made little difference. He seemed to manage just fine dipping into it here and there. But within three months he was up to the new limit. The strange thing is that if you had asked him what he had spent the money on, he couldn't have told you. He hadn't bought a new car, he hadn't been on holiday... he hadn't even bought a new television. He had just spent it on 'stuff'. But the fact of the matter was that the money was gone and he had nothing to show for it.

And then the bank increased his limit again. By now he knew he was on a slippery slope. He tried to be disciplined and he was good for a while. It was tough, but he didn't let his fingers touch that increased balance. But when the credit card company sent him some blank cheques, his will of iron crumbled and he couldn't resist them… they were just so easy to use.

Fourteen months down the line and he now owed them almost £10,000. All the while he was making the minimum monthly repayment.

One month he couldn't even make the minimum payment. He knew it had always been just a matter of time. But then it seemed as if fate had intervened. Another credit card company contacted him to see if he was interested in transferring the balance from his credit card to theirs at 0% interest for six months. No interest whatsoever? This seemed too good to be true! He wasted no time in transferring the debt across to the new card.

If he had been wiser, more disciplined, or if he had guessed even a fraction of the pain that lay ahead, Carl would at least have cut the old card in two. But he didn't. And now he had two credit cards: one with a £10,000 debt on it and another that had a £10,000 limit… and not a penny owing on it.

You don't have to be Einstein to work out what happened next. You may think he was naïve – maybe you're right. But we can all be a little naïve from time to time. I have seen many people do what Carl did. All kinds of people. He 'maxed out' both cards – and then used a new card to pass the debt along.

Over the next three years he accumulated eight cards with over £40,000 of debt; his interest payment alone was £8,000 a year – over two-thirds of his take-home pay.

Amazingly, the offers of new loans and credit cards kept coming thick and fast. But things had spiralled so far out of control that by now Carl wasn't borrowing to spend; he was increasing his debt to meet the minimum payments on the old cards.

And then one day Carl made the mistake of missing a mortgage payment on his home so that he could make the payments on his credit cards. The next month he missed another, then another. The letter threatening to take his home arrived from the building society at ten o'clock on the Tuesday morning that he died.

When they found him in the garage, he had left a note to his family apologizing for letting them down, but he thought there was no way out and he was so very sorry.

I wanted to tell you Carl's story because, sadly, it's all too common. I have seen many people who felt like Carl did on that Tuesday morning. Someone reading this book may even be considering doing what he did. Even if you have made some mistakes along the way, the banks, building societies and credit card companies bear some blame as well. Debt can make people feel very alone, even foolish and at rock bottom. Remember, this is not just you and you can get through this. Don't let it all crowd in on you as Carl did.

You can come through this.

Chapter 4

The Magic of Credit Cards – And the Tricks They Play on You

Credit cards are big business. It's hard to remember life without them. Pretty much wherever we are in the world, we can buy whatever we want and not have to worry about paying for it until some while later. It's true that there are some advantages to using them (such as the extra protection you get if you pay for goods with your credit card), but the problem is that we no longer have to think about whether we actually need the item or even if we can afford it. Credit cards lull us into a false world in which everything is readily available and we can have what we want, when we want it. They make us believe that the money we are spending is not 'real' money. They feed the 'buy it now' culture that has become a way of life, because in truth it is far easier to pay by plastic than to part with our hard-earned cash.

However useful they are, the truth is that credit cards have been at the root of much misery, sadness and pain. This is probably why the Chief Executive of one of the major banks that owns a credit card business said he would never let his kids use them.[5] I have seen homes lost, families broken and lives ruined by a chain of events that simply began with a credit card taken out with the best of intentions. In the second half of 2007, more than five million people missed a payment on their credit card. The resulting bank charges totalled around £61 million.[6]

For most of the people I have come into contact with at the debt counselling centre, credit cards have become a way of life. In fact, it's scary just how many people believe that the 'available balance' detailed on their credit card statement is *their* money to spend in the same way as if they were in credit in their current account. Credit cards are being used to pay for everyday expenses such as groceries. And the result is that large chunks of monthly pay cheques are being swallowed up to meet the ever-increasing minimum credit card payment. Many people never pay the full balance, just the minimum payments, and have no idea just how long it will take to repay the debt. I often come across people who have no idea of the rate of interest they are paying. The amount of interest I see on people's monthly statements is, to put it mildly, totally frightening. Many people have numerous credit cards, each with hefty balances. When I ask what they've spent this money on, few can remember and most say something along the lines of, 'Oh, I don't know, just this and that.'

At the moment, the credit card companies are running adverts that tell us that cash is rubbish and credit cards are magic. Well, if they are magic, it may be useful to wise up a little on some of the tricks the magicians from the credit card companies use.

1. The 0% interest rate

A phrase I hear all too often is 'I took that card out to pay off my debts'. Many people take on fresh debt as a way of keeping up the payments on old debt. This is when matters truly begin to spiral out of control. So often it is the result of what I believe to be one of the major credit card traps – the lure of the 0% interest rate.

I remember one young woman who came to the centre for advice who had £2,000 of debt on one credit card. Previously she had decided to transfer her balance on her old card (which had a high rate of interest) to a credit card which promised to charge no interest for the first six months. She made two errors which, in all fairness to her, are very common mistakes. First, she was attracted by the offer of 0% interest for the first six months – who wouldn't be? But she had not considered what would happen if she had not cleared the balance before the introductory rate expired. She had only made a very small dent in the debt before the six months were up, not least because she had been using those months as a breather rather than an impetus to clear her debt. She was back onto a high rate of interest.

Secondly, like so many others, rather than cutting up the first credit card, she had continued to use it. And so it was not long before she had two credit cards, both of which had been maxed out and had high interest rates. She had failed to gain any benefit from the interest-free period and was now in a worse position than six months ago.

Yet she had still believed that the key to overcoming her financial burden lay in using the interest-free periods to her advantage. And so she'd continued with her strategy of taking out cards with similar deals. This carried on until one day she realized things had to change. That morning, when she woke up, she could barely lift herself out of bed because of the immense depression she was under as a result of her debt – now a staggering £32,000! That was when she picked up the telephone and made an appointment to see me for advice.

Everyone is susceptible to these traps, regardless of status and income. The news recently featured the story of Ed Mitchell, former BBC, ITN and Sky News reader. Before his financial difficulties, he was earning £100,000 a year. With debts of £250,000, he said that his financial problems had stemmed from him using one credit card to pay off another.[7]

2. Credit card companies love late payers

I'm going to surprise you now by telling you that credit card companies love people who pay late! But when you think about it, you can see why. It is these people who really make them their money. There are two types of credit card users: the convenience users – those who usually pay the balance off at the end of every month – and what the credit card companies call 'revolvers', who often pay late, only make the minimum payments and regularly miss payments. Without the revolvers, the profit margins of the credit industry would be far less healthy – to the tune of billions of pounds.

Before the 'Credit Crunch', credit card companies used to court the business of those with poor credit on a daily basis – and then charge them an outrageous interest rate. Just think of the offers that used to bombard thousands upon thousands of letterboxes each morning: 'You have been specially selected to apply for our premier credit card!' A high percentage of those finding one of these offers on their doormat would have had a poor credit rating. And yet ironically it would be to the delight of the credit card company if they were persuaded to apply for a card. They knew they could make money out of these guys. At the advice centre I met many people like this, who were so pleased to be wanted by the credit card company that they didn't look at the rate of interest they would be charged.

Conversely, convenience users were not so welcome to credit card companies. One man was even turned down for a card with a major credit card company because of his good credit rating![8] We have seen companies cancelling the credit cards of thousands of their customers, but not because they don't pay their loans on time – these people pay off the full balance at the end of every month. But for the credit card companies, that's the problem – they just don't make enough money out of these financially wise people.

3. The minimum payment

So what's the big deal about only making the minimum payment on your credit card each month? Well, this is the dream scenario for the credit industry. Imagine you use a credit card which charges 19% interest per year to buy a T-shirt costing £14.50; you've got other debts on the card and you only make the minimum 3% payment each month. The outcome is frightening. It will take you around fifteen years to pay for that T-shirt![9] This is because you would not only be paying 19% interest on the £14.50 but also the credit card company will be adding on 19% interest per year on the interest which has already built up – it's the power of compound interest!

4. Credit card cheques

You always need to be on your toes where your credit cards are concerned. One really common tactic is for the companies to send out blank cheques to their customers. It is so simple: you just have to complete the cheque and then it's yours to cash and spend. What a temptation!

I found out all about this when I met Sarah. She was a single parent who came to get advice. Her children were young and she was at home with them all day. She was in receipt of Income Support. She was struggling to make ends meet and was already up to her eyeballs in debt, living on credit just to get by. And then one of her credit card companies (she had five cards) began to send her these cheques each month. It seemed straightforward – she just had to fill out the amount she needed, sign the cheque and then cash it and the money was hers. She later said to me, 'I just wasn't thinking clearly at the time. I should've realized the cheques weren't going to help me in the long term but get me further and further into debt.' But she was feeling the pressure at the time. Her freezer was empty and needed stocking up, the children needed winter coats and with Christmas just around the corner, the adverts for the children's toys had already started to rub off on her children and the 'can I haves' had begun. Besides, Sarah thought that if the company had offered the cheques to her, they obviously felt she was in a position to repay the money. The truth is that you would need a will of iron not to act as Sarah did. The temptation is immense. But there is only one way to respond: bin them!

5. Increasing your credit limit

Another trick used by the credit card companies is to increase the limit on credit cards. One day a friend of mine noticed that her credit limit had been increased by £1,000 without the company even asking her if she wanted the increase. This was a difficult one. All that extra available credit and so many lovely things she could buy. But her sensible side dug its heels in and she telephoned the company straight away to request that the limit go back to its original amount. She knew she could not rely on her own self-discipline not to dip into that money! She now regularly checks her statements just to be sure that they have not stealthily increased her credit limit again.

6. Increasing the APR

Read the statements and letters you get in relation to your credit card very carefully. On 31 December 2007, people holding a Marbles credit card were paying 19.9% APR for retail purchases and 23.9% APR for cash withdrawals. On 1 January 2008, these rates increased to 26.9% and 33.9% respectively.[10] No doubt some cardholders were oblivious to this, as they did not read their letters and statements. And yet, the difference that interest rate rise made to most of those people was significant. (In fact, on a debt of £1,000 repaid over twelve months, the monthly payments when the interest rate is 19.9% will be approximately £99.92 and on an interest rate of 26.99%, the monthly payments will be £105.82. The overall difference paid is around £70.80.[11]) Other customers, even though aware of the change in the APR, will remain with Marbles because they cannot organize themselves to take out a different credit card with a more favourable rate. The cost of their disorganization will be immense and will produce large profits for the credit card company.

Yes, credit card companies are magicians; just don't let them make your money disappear!

SIXTY SECOND PAGE
THE MAGIC OF CREDIT CARDS
– AND THE TRICKS THEY PLAY
ON YOU

Credit cards whisper 'This is not real money.'

It's far easier to spend on a card than to use cash.

Take care with offers of 0% interest.

Credit card companies make their money from the late payers.

Don't just make the minimum payment.

Rip up credit card cheques.

Avoid temptation – reduce your credit limit.

Read your letters and statements from the credit card company carefully.

✓ The Price is Right! (... making sure!)

Attacking those utility bills!

• **Water**

Water is one thing none of us can do without and it seems that prices are steadily rising,[12] but there are some ways it might be possible to save the pennies. You may wish to consider a water meter being installed at your property. In doing so, you would only pay for the water that you actually use. As a rule of thumb, if you have fewer people than bedrooms in the house, a water meter could save you money. However, if the washing machine is always on, and the family is queuing up to use the shower, a water meter may not be the best option for you.

Contact your local water supplier and ask them to estimate whether you would save money in changing to a water meter. Remember that after having a water meter installed, you are usually given a grace period of up to one year to change your mind. Because of this, if you get a meter installed and don't end up saving any money, you can ask for the water meter to be removed.

If you have a water meter already, then consider how you can cut back further on your water usage – have a look at www.waterwise.org.uk for some inspiration. A friend of mine cut their annual water bill in half by changing to a water meter.

• Gas and electricity

Around four million households have never changed utility providers. However, by doing so, the average family of four could save around £250 per year. Eight out of ten households who have previously swapped suppliers could make further savings by switching again.[13]

• Always provide meter readings – if you receive an estimated bill, provide them with an up-to-date meter reading as soon as possible, otherwise you could get a nasty shock one day!

• Manage your account online rather than receiving paper bills – you will save money in doing so.

• Pay by monthly direct debit – this spreads the cost evenly over the year and means you are not stung with high payments in the winter months. There is often a small discount for direct debit payments as well.

• Consider duel fuel; that is, using the same provider for both gas and electricity. This may also save you money.

• Take a minute to check out www. energysavingtrust.org.uk. The energy saving tips could save you £250.[14]

• Check you are receiving value for money from your gas and electricity provider by shopping around (check out some of the websites mentioned

on page 39). **When you have chosen your new supplier, you will have to sign a consent form for the switch to take place and the supplier usually does the rest for you. Remember to take a meter reading before the switch.**

Chapter 5

Plastic Surgery!

In the previous chapter, we looked at some of the tricks used by the credit industry. By now you may well be thinking, 'I think I'd rather live without these cards. Millions of people before me have coped without plastic and I can too!' For you, it may be as simple as paying off the entire balance on your next credit card bill, cutting up the card and reverting to that method of payment which you thought was a relic to be found only in the museums: cash!

For others, however, it's just not that simple. Maybe you feel that your credit cards have got out of control and you just don't know where to begin to start tackling them. Well, fear not! It's going to take some willpower and sheer determination, but I believe that you can do it. The following radical steps are only for those for whom credit cards have become a major feature in trapping them in debt. These are extreme measures for extreme circumstances – but they work.

First, I want you to open your wallet and tip out your credit cards onto the kitchen table. Now take a pair of scissors and cut each card up into tiny pieces. (Some companies ask their employees to use a credit card for business purposes to keep track of expenses – it may be best not to decimate that one!) If nothing else is achieved, this in itself will make it pretty difficult for you to continue spending. I understand that this may cause you considerable pain. These cards have been a part of your life! But, if you are intent on ridding yourself of debt, it is non-negotiable. You will never overcome debt if you continue to use the cards.

If you really must keep one card – 'just in case' – then I want to make it as difficult as possible for you to actually use it. Take the card, place it in a plastic bag and put the bag in a container filled with water. Then place the container in the freezer. Within a few hours, the card will be imprisoned in a block of ice. If you are ever overcome by temptation, the card will not be in your wallet ready for swiping without you having to give any thought to two important questions: 'Can I afford it?' and 'Do I need it?'

On the contrary, you will have plenty of time to consider whether you really ought to buy that new outfit while you wait for the block of ice to defrost. (By the way, I recently read somewhere that your microwave and the magnetic strip on the back of your credit card are unlikely to hit it off. So don't try to speed along the defrosting process!)[15]

If credit cards have led you into too much debt, then cutting them up is definitely a good idea. But how we deal with these outstanding balances will differ depending on our circumstances. For those so heavily in debt they can only just think of paying the priority creditors, credit cards are way down the list of those to pay. But others will find after doing their budget and making a few savings that they have some money spare to attack their credit card balances. If that's you then this is how you do it – and it's called snowballing.

First, gather together the most recent statement for each of your credit cards. Take a sheet of paper and list each card, noting down its outstanding balance and the rate of interest being charged. It will look something like this:

Name of card	Amount outstanding	Rate of interest
Card 1	£850	23.00%
Card 2	£340	29.90%
Card 3	£1,000	17.00%
Card 4	£1,250	18.00%

You are now going to begin the process of knocking each card dead, one by one. This is how it's done.

First, make the minimum repayment on all your cards except for the one with the highest rate of interest. Pay any extra available income towards that card, over and above the minimum payment.

This will be a good time to use the budget that you prepared in Chapter 2. Be ruthless with yourself. Could you do without the weekly takeaway or cut back on that all-singing all-dancing television package for the time being? This will give you more money to plough into your credit cards. And let's face it – the faster those suckers are paid off, the less interest you pay and the less money you are throwing into the hands of the credit card company!

Keep all these payments going until that first card has been repaid in full – and let me tell you, it's going to be satisfying!

The next part of our action plan is to go back to your list and see which is your next most expensive card. As before, in addition to the minimum payment you have been making on it, throw at it all of the money you were paying on the first card. At the same time, continue to make the minimum payments on the remaining cards.

This process is often referred to as 'snowballing your credit cards'. If you stick at it, one by one you will wipe out those cards – what a liberating experience!

Are you ready for the final challenge of the chapter? Go to the freezer, remove the plastic container housing the surviving credit card and place it on your kitchen worktop. Return a few hours later, remove the card from the water, take a pair of scissors and cut it into tiny pieces.

Congratulations! You have now dealt with your credit card debt and removed all temptation to pay by plastic.

Debit Cards

Finally, a word or two here about debit cards. Debit cards are very different from credit cards. Rather than being sent a bill at the end of the month for any goods purchased, the money is taken from your bank account straight away. With Solo and Electron debit cards, the balance on your account is checked before each transaction. As a result, if there are insufficient funds in your account then the transaction will not go through. However, with Switch, Visa and Delta, the account is not necessarily checked before the transaction is completed. The result is that you may not always have enough money in your account to cover the purchase and you could then be stung with hefty charges for going overdrawn. But there's no denying it – debit cards are very convenient. Just remember, although on the face of it they seem less 'dangerous' than credit cards, it's still much easier to spend on them than it is to use cash. It always hurts more to spend with our hard-earned cash than it does to pay by plastic!

In the next chapter, I will introduce you to something truly radical – 'back to cash'. Here is the key to regaining financial control.

SIXTY SECOND PAGE PLASTIC SURGERY!

Cut up your credit cards.

List the outstanding balances and rates of interest on each card.

Make the minimum payments on all the cards except the card with the highest rate of interest. Pay all extra available cash into this card.

Continue to do this until the card has been paid off in full.

Repeat this process with the card with the next highest rate of interest until that card has also been paid off.

Keep going in the same way until all the cards are wiped out.

Chapter 6

Back to Cash

Have you ever wondered where all your money goes? I think most of you will recognize the situation where you're drawing near the end of the month, pay day is approaching (although not quickly enough!) and your bank account is nearly running on empty. Every month you can't believe how fast your money has slipped through your fingers and how little you have to show for it. It's an all too familiar picture for many. I believe there are major reasons why these days it's so much easier to lose control of our finances.

Try to imagine life a couple of generations back when the summers were long and hot, the Christmases were white and credit cards didn't exist. If you saw something you wanted to buy and didn't have the cash on you at the time, you simply couldn't buy it. Yes, you could pop to the bank to make a withdrawal or walk home to get the money, but the more likely scenario was that you would wait until you were next in town and ensure that you had the money on you then. This meant that every purchase involved an element of planning and consideration that the birth of credit cards seems to have removed from our thought processes altogether. In fact, an advertisement for the very first credit card had as its slogan, 'Take the waiting out of wanting'. The problem with this is that it can stop us asking those two absolutely vital questions: Do I need it? Can I afford it?

I wonder why credit cards cause us to skip asking those questions. Perhaps somewhere amongst its make-up of plastic, magnetic strip and chip and pin is firmly planted a little voice that whispers to us, 'This is not real money!' When we stick something on the credit card, it can seem like ages before we have to start even thinking about parting with our hard-earned cash. And it's for these very reasons that one expert said that most people end up spending about a third more when they use credit cards.[16]

So I'm setting you a challenge. It's called 'Cash for a Month', and as the name suggests, your task is to live without your credit cards for a whole month! It may seem like returning to the Dark Ages, but even if the experience takes you back in time, I promise that it will take you forward in getting in control of your spending.

For day-to-day spending, you will simply be using cash – your credit cards will not be seeing the light of day for the next month.

Let me show you how this will work:

• Leave bank standing orders and direct debits unchanged. Those will go through your account in the normal way.

• At the beginning of the week, work out sensibly what money you will need for the week ahead.

• Go to the cashpoint and withdraw that amount in cash. (It's important that you withdraw all the money in one go, as it's easy to lose control by making regular visits to the cashpoint.)

• Take the cash home and divide it amongst different envelopes marked according to your categories of spending. For example, you may have worked out that you need £50 for food, £30 for socializing and £20 for travel.

• As you go through the week, use the money you have withdrawn to meet your various living expenses.

There will be times when you want to buy something that you haven't planned for that week. This will require you to ask yourself a question that previous generations had to ask themselves – do I have the cash to pay for it? Imagine that you see a CD that you want to buy but haven't budgeted for. One of two things is going to happen here: you either have to wait until next week and put it in the budget (by which time you've had a whole week to think about it and may well have changed your mind); or if you have got some cash on you, you buy it. But because you have not factored the CD into your budget, then this will mean cutting back somewhere else if that cash is going to last you to the end of the week.

One woman who tried out 'Cash for a Month' wrote to me and said, 'I was in the supermarket gaily throwing things into the trolley and then about halfway around the shop I thought, "Hang on a minute – have I got enough money on me to pay for all this stuff?" I can tell you that I started throwing things in a lot more slowly after that. And when the girl at the checkout told me how much it had come to, it was much less than my normal bill. She said, "You look pleased!" I replied, "Well, I've just discovered cash!" She looked bemused, but not as bemused as I used to look waiting to see how much was going to hit my credit card!'

Another couple who tried 'Cash for a Month' said that on the Saturday of their first week they decided to go to the cinema. The husband was really looking forward to seeing the latest Batman film. He was about to get on the phone and book the tickets on his credit card as he normally did when his wife said, 'Hang on a second, how much are the tickets?' He replied, '£13 for the two plus a £1.50 booking fee'. She said, 'How much have we got in the "entertainment kitty?"' He rummaged for an envelope in a drawer, opened it and then his face fell. '£5.82,' he said. They hired a DVD.

Doing the 'Cash for a Month' challenge will provide

you with a real picture of exactly where your money is going. It will no longer be disappearing into a big black hole, but you should be able to account for pretty much every penny – imagine that!

Accept the 'Cash for a Month' challenge – and suddenly you're in control again!

Look after the pennies...

• Make a shopping list and stick to it!

• Don't automatically renew your annual travel insurance – renew it just before you are going on holiday. Do you even need an annual policy?

• Take a packed lunch to work or college – it's surprising how much buying lunch every day adds up to.

• Request regular bank statements as frequently as possible without incurring extra charges (online statements are free anyway). This will help you to keep on top of what you have in your account. Always read and check your bank statements carefully.

• Walk/cycle more.

• If you have two cars in your family, consider whether you really need them both. Do your waistline and your bank balance a favour and get a bike.

• If you have a mobile phone, consider whether you would have more control if you were on Pay As You Go (although contracts can be cheaper).

• Check out the 'spendometer' on Credit Action's website, www.creditaction.org.uk. This can be downloaded onto your mobile phone at no cost. Using this facility, you can set your own weekly or monthly budget and can also break this down into different categories of spending such as food, clothes and entertainment. If you go over your budget, it even lets you know!

• Don't always accept the price you're offered – negotiate!

I've got a friend who negotiates on nearly everything he buys. I've lost count of the times I have heard him utter the words, 'What's the best price you can do that for?' The more he does it, the more inspired he becomes to have another crack at it. It's just amazing what he saves and what freebies he manages to get thrown in. He boasts about the thousands upon thousands of pounds he has saved over the years just by asking if there is any leeway on the price. This has worked for houses, holidays, hotels, cars, telephone packages, suits, even down to hiring sunbeds on a beach in Spain. He is living proof that there is certainly some truth in the old adage: if you don't ask, you don't get!

Chapter 7

When the Going Gets Tough, the Tough Go Shopping

We've all been there. We pop to the shops to get a new bag for work and come home minus the bag but having managed to pick up a couple of tops that we just couldn't leave in the shop. Those tops were 'absolute must-have/every wardrobe needs them/these are so going to improve my image' tops. Maybe we even convinced ourselves that we deserved a treat after such a hard week in the office. And yet, as I write, one of them is hanging in your wardrobe, tags still firmly attached (and that's only if you've remembered to take it out of the plastic shopping bag!).

In fact, there is now a recognized compulsive shopping disorder, oniomania, which we might know as 'retail therapy' – which leads people to binge shop and can result in them getting into thousands of pounds of debt. Researchers have declared that anti-depressants can help to reduce the compulsive shopping tendency.[17] Some people would say that shopping makes them feel better. It is a pick-me-up, but the high is usually short-lived and has often long faded by the time the shopper gets home. The shopping bag may be dumped in the hallway or on the bedroom floor and is already forgotten. That is, until the credit card statement comes through our letterbox, or we rediscover the shopping bag and guiltily peer inside to recall the item that we are no longer bothered about but cannot return, because the twenty-eight day return period has passed.

Don't get me wrong; there's no harm in treating ourselves every so often, but if we regularly buy things we don't use or need, it may be worth considering why. Sometimes there may be unresolved issues that retail therapy may briefly smooth over but will certainly not resolve. One woman put it very well: 'Retail therapy is the equivalent of a throat lozenge when what we need is ointment for the soul.'[18]

Compulsive shopping can play serious havoc with the control we have over our money. In the television series *Sex and the City*, one of the characters, Carrie, realizes that she can't afford to remain in her apartment after going crazy on shopping sprees. She says, 'I've spent $40,000 on shoes and I have no place to live? I will literally be the old woman who lived in her shoes!'[19]

If you find the pull of retail therapy difficult to resist,

try these top tips.

• Only carry cash with you. It's simple – if you don't have enough cash on you, you can't buy the item. This one tip will transform our relationship with shopping – it says 'there are limits'. Think about how much of this month's pay you want to spend.

• Take a list with you when you go shopping and discipline yourself to stick to the list.

• Give yourself a 'cooling-off' period. This could be one day for small items and perhaps two weeks or even a month for larger purchases. Work out what your cooling-off period will be for all items and stick to it. If you see something you want, make a note of it in your diary. If you still want it after the cooling-off period, then consider purchasing it – but even then, only if you can afford it and haven't been able to get a better deal by shopping around. Who knows, by that time the desperation to own the latest gadget may well have subsided!

• Ask yourself not only whether you *want* the item but if you really *need* it.

• If the temptation to buy is too great, limit your shopping trips and your visits to Internet shopping sites.

• Consider how the purchase would impact your budget. Will you have to do without something else

if you buy it? This may be a very persuasive tool!
The desperation to own the item may be somewhat
diluted if in order to buy it you would have to forego
a night out with friends.

One area that can certainly be hard to keep tabs on is
supermarket shopping. One lady told me that she feels
out of control in the supermarket. I confess I have some
sympathy with her. In fact I have a recurring dream:

*I am at the supermarket checkout and I'm piling the
goodies from my trolley onto the conveyor belt. How
I managed to fit this lot into that trolley is anybody's
guess! Well, even if I say so myself, I seem to have
mastered the art of balancing the food so that,
although it towers above the rim of the trolley, it does
not crash to the floor as I run the gauntlet from the
final aisle to the checkout.*

*And so here I am using that same technique to cram
it all onto the conveyor belt. Why does it always look
so much more when it's spread out in all its glory for
everyone to see? The man behind me with his measured
basket of a few bits and bobs looks agitated at the
amount I'm buying and no doubt the length of time it's
all going to take. (So, if he's got a problem why didn't
he go to the 'baskets only' queue?) I can hear the little
boy helping his mother at the next checkout whispering,
'Look how much that lady's buying, Mum!'*

And that familiar hot feeling of panic passes over

me. How much is all this going to cost? I can't even remember chucking some of these items into the trolley. What was going through my mind when I chose the jar of octopus in oil? How long is it going to take me to work through those four tins of tuna? (Even if they are part of the BOGOF deal!) More to the point, can I face the prospect of having to eat my way through that lot before the 'best before' date is up?

Then my eye falls on the steaks. They are fillets and they are on special offer and they do look so delicious. But under the bright lights of the checkout, they still seem rather expensive. Rather embarrassed, I say to the young Saturday girl, 'Actually I've realized I don't need those steaks,' and she puts them to one side.

I'm rushing to bag everything while the young girl appears to be setting a world record for the speed at which she is able to scan each item. I just can't keep up and soon I am up to my neck in tins of Heinz baked beans, toilet rolls and bags of pasta. And the man behind is looking ever more impatient.

I glance at the conveyor belt and know that the dreaded moment is looming. The final item, a bag of broccoli, is weighed and I'm feeling really flushed. Why didn't I make a budget and a list, and then I wouldn't be waiting with such fear for the girl to announce how much I have spent?

She keeps hitting the keys of the till furiously and finally looks at me with blood dripping from her lips and says, 'Forty thousand, three hundred pounds and ten pence!'

The truth is that sometimes the dream came pretty near reality (OK, not the blood and not £40,000, but still scary), and I had to do something. I decided to do the shop online. That way, I could see exactly how much I was spending and I felt totally in control. I also had a hunch that the tactics used by the supermarkets (like that wonderful smell of bread to make me feel hungry) might not have such an effect on me when I'm sitting at my computer at home as they would if I was traipsing the aisles.

I used the website www.mysupermarket.com, which I mentioned on page 29. Not only was I able to avoid the stressful experience of going to the supermarket, but the website checked whether I was getting the most out of my money. It looked at my trolley and offered me alternative similar products from within the store I had chosen that were 'equal in quality but lower in price'. It also told me that I could buy an almost identical trolley-load of goods at one of the other stores more cheaply. I was able to swap my trolley over to the cheaper store totally hassle-free. The difference between the cheapest and the most expensive trolley saved me a bomb!

Planning our spending (rather than just letting it happen) is one of the keys to staying in financial control. Trust me, it's far kinder to the purse and to the heart. And I'm sleeping a little easier!

P.S. If you are really finding it hard to resist the purchase, try a little technique that always makes me think twice.

It's called 'Money Equivalent Labour'. In other words, do a quick calculation as to how many hours you have to work to pay for that 'must-have'. Of course it all depends on your income but it's pretty scary anyway. If you earn £13,000 a year you have to work almost five and a half hours to pay for that £30 top (three hours if you're on £26,000 a year) and seventy hours for that £400 television (that's nearly forty hours if you're on £26,000 a year).

That normally does the trick!

SIXTY SECOND PAGE
WHEN THE GOING GETS TOUGH,
THE TOUGH GO SHOPPING

Budget
Know what your budget is for the shopping
trip and stick to it – don't be afraid to carry a
calculator around with you.

Make a list
Write down exactly what you are going to buy
and keep strictly to it. If you want something
that's not on the list, trade it for something that
is. As you shop, if something is more expensive
than anticipated, choose a cheaper alternative or
remove something else from the list.

Be realistic
Don't always fall for the BOGOF ('Buy One, Get
One Free'), or 'three for the price of two' deals.
Yes, you are always going to need toilet rolls, but
if you've got a cupboard full of Andrex Supersoft
already, maybe your budget would be more
wisely spent on something else this week.

Recognize the power of impulse buying.
Impulse buying is one of the main contributors
to debt.

Trauma at the Hole in the Wall

Picture the scene. It's a Tuesday night and Sam is on his way out for a get-together with his friends at the local pub. He has spent a while sprucing himself up because you never know who you will bump into. He checks his wallet and realizes that he's all out of cash again and will need to stop off at the cash point on the way. He can't believe he's already spent all that money that he withdrew yesterday afternoon. Where did it go? Anyway, he joins the queue, but then starts to worry whether he's actually got any money in his account to withdraw. He remembers that a bank statement arrived the other morning, but he'd binned it without even taking it out of its envelope.

And then it's his turn. He puts his card in and as always he starts muttering under his breath, 'Oh please, oh please, oh please,' just hoping that he will have some available credit. He always seems to be in overdraft these days. He can hardly remember the last time he was in funds in his current account. He dares not check his balance. On some of the cashpoint machines it flashes up on the screen once it has given you your cash, but he always looks away. Tonight he is definitely not in the mood for looking the tiger in the eye. Why spoil what he is hoping will be a good evening? He is just grateful it paid out the £30 he'd requested. Why does pay day seem to come around so slowly?

The trauma at the hole in the wall is a scenario which is all too familiar to many people. Sam is losing financial control – that is, if it's not already been lost. Maybe you can empathize with that panic he felt as he stood face to face with the cash point. Have you got to the stage where you too are never sure if the cashpoint is going to pay out? You use your overdraft as if it is your money to spend. Rather than looking at your account which is £500 overdrawn and working out how you can repay that £500, you look at the £750 overdraft limit and are pleased that you still have £250 to spend. All of these are signs that you may not have a firm grip on your finances.

If you find yourself going red in the face at a hole in the wall, you may suffer from 'cashpoint blood pressure'. It's one of the classic symptoms of a terrible illness called 'financiallyoutofcontrolitis'. Here are some other symptoms:

• Not being sure whether the cashpoint machine is going to pay out or not.

• Not being at all sure what figure will be at the end of a bank statement.

• Always being overdrawn.

• Losing track of the direct debits or standing orders that are operating on your account.

• Losing cash around the house or finding odd bits of cash – even bank notes – in various pockets.

• Readily borrowing from and lending money to friends.

• Impulse buying.

• Instead of asking, 'What is the total cost?' asking, 'Can I afford the monthly repayment?'

• Making minimum payments each month on credit cards.

• Not knowing the rate of interest you are paying on credit cards, store cards and bank borrowings.

• Getting taken in by offers of finance that come through the post.

• Leaving payment of bills until the last possible moment, certainly until the 'red' bill – and often not until threatened with legal action.

They're all key symptoms to watch out for. Any of it feel all too familiar to you? Well, don't ignore it – get your financial health back!

Look after the pennies...

• Cut down on alcohol – your liver will be pleasantly surprised!

• Cancel your gym membership and exercise in the great outdoors.

• If possible, pay for insurance policies in one lump sum rather than opting for the usually more expensive instalment plan.

• Use energy-saving light bulbs – they may be more expensive initially but on average one bulb will save you £7 per year on your bills. Multiply this by the number of light bulbs in your home and you can see the difference it would make.[20]

• Eat fewer convenience foods – these are always more expensive than making meals from scratch (OK, so not every night – but at least sometimes!).

• Don't be afraid of 'own brand' products – they are often as good as branded ones.

• Don't leave appliances on standby – it is estimated that an average family could save £37 each year by turning appliances off rather than leaving them on standby.[21]

• Do your gift shopping in the sales (but perhaps not Christmas shopping in the January sales – it's so boring and, anyway, by the time Christmas comes you can't remember where you put the things).

• Set up a standing order into a savings account each month for long-term savings and recurring expenses.

• Consider downgrading your television package.

Chapter 8

Home Sweet Home: Saving Your House from Repossession

Andy and Jane are sat with me in my tiny office. Jane is emotional and tearful and Andy can't look me in the eye. He seems ashamed. He is sat hunched over and his eyes are fixed on his trainers. They both look weary; weary from lack of sleep and weary of life. They start to tell me about their situation. Jane does the talking. They have two young children and another on the way. They live in a modest house. They've never been what most people would consider 'well-off', but they've always managed. Jane spends most of her time looking after the kids but does some part-time work at the local primary school. Until recently Andy had a well-paid job working as a salesman. Then just before Christmas he was made redundant. This really hit them hard – and not just financially. Andy is now suffering from depression, which is making it a lot more difficult for him to find a new job – although, Jane quickly assures me, he really is trying.

Their biggest worry at the moment is their mortgage. They were coping just fine before but with the loss of the main wage, things have now become a struggle. They were unable to meet last month's payment and the next payment is due in two weeks. They have seen so many stories in the news about the increase of repossessions and frankly they are beside themselves with worry. What will happen to them? Will they find someone from the bank on their doorstep one morning ready to change the locks? Where will they go? And with that, Jane just breaks down in tears.

I hand Jane some tissues and assure them that this cannot happen. Yes, this is a serious situation and needs prompt action. But no one will be changing the locks and asking them to leave the property without a court order. And they will have a fair opportunity to resolve the situation before it gets that far. At the end of the day, even if they do end up in the county court, no judge *wants* to see anyone lose their home. This would be an absolute last resort.

I urge them to pull their chairs up closer and we sit together around the table and start to work through their financial details. At the moment, with Andy being out of work, they simply cannot afford the normal monthly payment. However, rather than making no payments at all I advise them to pay what they can for the time being, however small an amount – even £50. They didn't realize that it was possible to do this and agree that straight after our appointment, they will go into the bank and make a payment.

Actually, the bank had already written to Andy and Jane about the missed payment, asking them to get in touch. Due to sheer fear, they had not done this. It becomes evident that they are finding it difficult to face up to the situation. I've no doubt they are just praying that this is all a bad dream and that everything will go away. I assure them that they are not alone in this. In fact, some people even wait until they receive a court summons for possession of the property before they decide it is time to see me for advice. I tell them just how important it is not to ignore a lender when they contact you. Nothing frustrates lenders more than being kept in the dark by elusive customers who just refuse to speak to them. Besides, there are a number of ways that they may actually be able to help borrowers who are in difficulty. These options are all worth exploring before the matter gets to court. (More on this later!)

Even if you have ignored the mortgage company for some time, it is never too late to contact them. Get in touch, advise them of your recent change in circumstances and start making whatever payments you can.

Andy's difficulties were at a very early stage. The big hurdle he had to overcome was simply picking up the phone and talking to his lender. He then needed to start to pay what he could, however little. If Andy had been renting his home, my advice would have been the same – talk to the landlord and start to pay something. But sometimes things have gone a lot further, actually into court proceedings. Even if you are in this situation, it's still not too late to save your home. Let's look at this next.

For me, the most poignant example I came across of someone about to lose their home was the story of Tom. Tom was married with two children. He and his wife kept separate bank accounts and he was in charge of paying the mortgage from his account. But Tom had a gambling problem and the mortgage had not been paid for many months. He had been intercepting the post for some time and his wife was completely in the dark. When he came to see me for advice, he presented me with a Notice of Eviction. The mortgage arrears had become so serious that the lender now had a date and time when they would take possession of the property, the family would have to leave their home and the locks would be changed.

This grown man who sat before me wept. He was afraid to tell his wife.

I telephoned the lender to inform them that we would be helping Tom to apply to suspend this eviction. Between then and the court date, he paid as much as he could afford towards the arrears.

I met Tom in the waiting room of the court at 9.45 a.m., just before the hearing. The situation was incredibly tense. If our application was not successful, then at 11.30

a.m. the bailiffs would attend at his home and change the locks. He had still not told his wife and children, who were now in work and school, totally oblivious to what was about to happen. He had secretly packed a bag of clothes for each of them, in the event that when they returned from work and school the house was no longer theirs. I had advised him to have some alternative arrangements in place just in case.

And then the moment arrived. His name was called and he rose from his chair in the waiting room, his face filled with terror. We entered the judge's chambers knowing that in fifteen minutes, Tom's life could be turned upside-down. The judge was firm yet fair. Of course he was not going to pat him on the back for missing the payments; it was only right that he should be chided in some way – he had a responsibility to pay the mortgage and he had let it slip – but he was given credit for the fact that he had now started to take the matter in hand. He had taken advice and had begun to make additional payments making inroads into clearing the arrears. The judge made an order for Tom to pay a certain amount each month towards the arrears in addition to the normal monthly payment.

The eviction was not going ahead. The bags of packed clothes hidden at the back of the wardrobe in the spare room would not be needed. Tom had been given a break and he was so very grateful.

It's never too late to start to take action to save your home. Here are my top tips to avoid repossession:

Contact the lender

Speak to the lender straight away and don't bury your head in the sand – they don't like being kept in the dark. Tell them that you are seeking legal advice. They may even be able to offer some solutions such as:

• Agreeing to reduced payments or a payment break for a few months. This would provide you with some breathing space and reduce the pressure at this difficult time.

• Agreeing to convert the mortgage from repayment to interest only. This is normally only a temporary measure, as with an interest-only mortgage none of the capital (the money borrowed initially) is being repaid.

• Agreeing to 'capitalize the mortgage arrears'. This means that the arrears are added to the total amount you owe. In that sense, they are 'wiped out'. However, because of this you will either have to increase your monthly payments slightly or repay it all over a longer period.

If the matter goes to court, the judge will credit you for contacting the lender and not simply ignoring the situation.

Make a budget and work out what you can afford to pay towards the arrears

You need to know how much money you can throw at the mortgage arrears. The budget that we looked at in Chapter 2 will be a vital tool for this. Can you cut back on any non-essential spending to release some spare cash to pay off the arrears? This may involve cutting out some luxuries for a while – it may be tough to do but you need to focus on saving your home. You may need to show the court your budget to prove that you are paying all you can off your arrears.

Tell the lender how much you can afford to pay. Agree to pay only a realistic and affordable amount – it is better to have an agreement that is realistic and which can be maintained than one which will be broken. Start to pay the amount you have offered straight away.

Continue to pay as much as possible

Many people who are struggling to pay their mortgage simply stop making any payment whatsoever. However, it is essential that you pay as much as you can afford each month, even if it is a very small amount. This shows you are committed to the mortgage and will go some way to keeping the arrears down.

Prioritize the mortgage

Your mortgage is one of your most important debts. Other companies may be pressurizing you more than your lender. But remember to pay THEM FIRST (see Chapter 3) and pay what you can towards your mortgage before paying back other non-priority debts such as credit cards, store cards, catalogues and other unsecured loans (that is, not secured on your home). Remember that if you have a second mortgage on your home – perhaps after taking out a consolidation loan – you must treat this with the same importance as the first mortgage. Many people lose their homes because of arrears on their second mortgage.

Seek free legal advice
Make an appointment at a free legal advice centre as soon as possible. They will help you to prepare a budget and will negotiate with the lender on your behalf. They will also advise you about any other debts you may have.

Be organized
Don't ignore letters from your lender. Open them and read them carefully, as they could contain important information. If there is anything you don't understand, you could ask the lender or your legal advisor to explain it to you. Have a file where you can safely store all letters you receive from the lender and copies of all letters you send to the lender. You may need to show these to a court in the future.

Can you increase your income?

• Could you temporarily take on some extra work?

• Could you consider taking in a lodger? You can receive up to £4,250 a year for renting out a room in your home without paying tax. Take advice on this first as this could affect your entitlement to benefits. There may also be restrictions on this in your mortgage and home insurance.

• Check that you are receiving all relevant benefits – ask a free legal advice centre for a benefits check.

If you have a court hearing

Notify your legal advisor immediately if you receive court papers. They will help you to prepare for court. It is very important that you attend all court appointments, even if an agreement has been reached with the lender. If your advisor cannot go with you, some courts will have a duty solicitor who will be able to represent you. When you go to court, take with you proof of income, a copy of your personal budget and copies of all correspondence.

Have an idea in mind of an amount you can pay towards the arrears in addition to the current monthly instalment. At this stage, it will be up to the court, and not the lender, what amount you should repay. The lender will be hoping for the arrears to be cleared within one to two years but the court has the power to stretch the repayment of the arrears over the remaining term of the mortgage.

Consolidation loans – take care!

We will look at these fully later on but for now be wary of taking out a further loan to repay your mortgage arrears. Such loans are often advertised by celebrities on television and they make it all seem so easy. However, these loans can have high interest rates and will almost certainly be secured against your home. Very often people who take out a consolidation loan are increasing their amount of secured debt and putting their home at further risk. They have turned unsecured credit card debt, loans and overdrafts into a secured loan.

If, after advice, you decide you cannot afford to remain in your home:

• Don't hand the keys back to the lender without first obtaining legal advice. Your responsibility to make the mortgage payments only stops once the house has been sold. If the sale of the property does not clear the amount that you owe to the mortgage company, you will be responsible for repaying any shortfall.

• Although it's a big step, it may be worth considering downsizing your home or moving to a cheaper area. This could significantly reduce your monthly mortgage payments and relieve some of the financial pressure. It's much better to sell your house yourself than to have the property repossessed. I can guarantee that, when you're in control, it will be much less stressful and is likely to be far less expensive than if the lender is calling the shots. If the lender repossesses your home, although they are under an obligation to obtain a reasonable price for the house, it will often be sold at auction where, in reality, it will achieve a much lower sale price. The downside of selling your home yourself is that it could affect your ability to be re-housed by the council, so you do need to take advice before you do anything.

• Obtain advice on re-housing options. Speak to a free legal advice centre or the housing section at your local council.

• If you are considering a mortgage rescue scheme, take care! Some councils, local authorities and lenders have mortgage rescue schemes which allow you to continue living in your home as tenant/part-tenant/part-owner if you are unable to afford the mortgage payments. Although they can enable you to remain in your home, they can also increase the overall level of your debt. Be wary of the privately run mortgage rescue schemes they are not regulated and often give you very little protection from eviction once you have sold the property.[22]

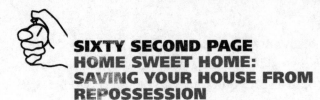

SIXTY SECOND PAGE
HOME SWEET HOME: SAVING YOUR HOUSE FROM REPOSSESSION

Pay what you can.

Contact the lender.

Get advice from a free legal advice agency.

Consider the possibility of a payment break, changing to interest-only payments or adding the arrears to your original loan.

Attend all court hearings.

Make your mortgage payment a priority.

Read and keep safe all letters.

Think about downsizing your home.

Take advice before handing back the keys to your house.

Be wary of taking a consolidation loan to repay arrears.

Chapter 9

Why Carol Vorderman is Not Necessarily Right

You're lying in bed enveloped in the duvet and you feel rough. You've been off work sick for a couple of days now but you've just got to get yourself well as soon as possible as that project which must be submitted by Friday is still sat on your desk in its infancy. And yet your head continues to pound as though you've done three rounds with Mike Tyson. Well, you may as well see what's on the box, and you painfully stretch for the remote control and start flicking through the channels to see which trashy daytime programme is going to keep you company for the next hour or so.

And then a familiar face appears on the screen. It's Carol Vorderman. She's attractive, animated and obviously incredibly intelligent. She's promising to solve all your debt problems. Your debts will be rolled into one (a consolidation loan) and you will only be required to make one simple payment each month. Wow, it all sounds so easy! There is the bit at the end about 'only homeowners need apply', but that shouldn't be a problem as you bought your place a couple of years ago. As you lie there, huddled under the duvet, you feel a sense of relief that this really could be the end of all of your financial worries. This woman is bright and clearly knows what she's talking about; and if she's promoting it, it's bound to be good.

Of course when you are up to your eyes in debt and paying Tom, Dick, Harry and all their friends, it can seem like a great idea to roll all your debts into one so that you just make the one payment each month. And yes, this can be a good thing. Sometimes it is sensible to consolidate your debts into a personal loan if the interest rate is lower than is being charged for your current debts. But there are a lot of ifs and buts.

If you take out a consolidation loan you may well use the money to wipe out the balances on your credit cards and overdraft. The only problem is that you'll need a will of iron to discipline yourself not to go on a mad shopping spree now that you have all of these available limits on your old credit cards. And if you do manage not to run up further debt, you will be in the minority because around three in five people who take out consolidation loans end up getting *deeper* into debt.[23]

Worse still, it's a condition of most consolidation loans

that they are secured against your home; that's why we so often hear the words 'only homeowners need apply'. This means that taking out a consolidation loan needs extremely careful consideration. Essentially, if you fall behind with the payments, you run the risk of losing your home. Any loan which is secured against your property is putting your house at risk. If you get into arrears (which can easily happen if your circumstances change), the lender can apply to the court to take your house from you in order to pay the loan off. Therefore, if you take out a loan which is secured on your property and pay off your credit cards with it, you are putting your house on the line. If your circumstances change and you can no longer afford the monthly payments on the loan, the lender can apply for possession of your home.

Let's consider the implications of this for a moment. You use your credit card to buy clothes and you later clear this credit card debt (along with other debts) by taking out a consolidation loan which is secured on your house. This means that the pair of trousers from Marks & Spencer is now effectively secured against your home in the same way as the money which you used to buy the house in the first place. Some people's homes have been repossessed because they took out a consolidation loan to repay credit card debts which arose from them buying clothes and holidays. They later could not keep up the payments on that loan and suddenly that shopping spree in Next and the holiday to Spain resulted in them losing their home.

If you are going for a consolidation loan, don't be tempted to borrow more money than you actually need. We've all seen the adverts that promise that your life will be changed once you take out a loan to pay off your debts and borrow that little bit extra to put in the bathroom suite or kitchen you've always wanted. To say they oversimplify matters is an understatement. It's as if the decision to borrow that extra £10,000 for the conservatory involves the same amount of thought as deciding which DVD you're going to hire this evening. In fact, I've no doubt many people actually do devote more time to the latter!

If you've considered all the options available to you, have taken advice and are still certain that a consolidation loan is the best option for you, then follow the golden rules on the next page.

SIXTY SECOND PAGE
WHY CAROL VORDERMAN IS NOT
NECESSARILY RIGHT

Take advice and make sure that a consolidation loan is the best option for you.

Don't borrow more than you need to pay off your debts.

Shop around for the best interest rate.

Spread the repayments over as short a period as possible.

Don't use consolidation loans which are secured against your home to pay off unsecured debt, for example credit card debt.

Remember that if you do decide to take out a consolidation loan to pay off your debts, you must avoid running up further debts – make sure you don't use the credit cards that now have zero balances on them.

Look after the pennies...

• Have two bank accounts: use one as a bill-paying account and the other as a spending account. This way you will always know that you have enough money to meet your bills and how much you have available to spend.

• If you have (and can afford) Internet access, get yourself set up with online banking. It is a really good way of keeping tabs on your finances, as you can check your account as often as you like.

• Don't put money into a savings account if you still owe it on credit cards and store cards. The interest you get on your savings is far less than the interest you are paying on your credit cards – so you will be losing money. Pay off your debts, then start saving. And if an emergency does arise before you've been able to start saving, you can always use your card then if you have to.

• Use extended warranties sparingly! These days appliances tend to be far more reliable. (OK, so as you're reading this you're waist-high in water in the kitchen because your washing machine has given up the ghost!) But really, how many times has your DVD player broken in the last few years? Consider putting the money you would have spent on a warranty into a savings account instead. This means that if your appliance does break down you can pay for the repairs or purchase a new one. And if it doesn't break down? Well, you're quids in!

• Be organized. Make a note in your diary of when bills need to be paid and pay them on time to avoid late fees.

DUMPING THE DEBT...

DO pay the priority debts first – these are the ones that matter the most, so remember to pay THEM FIRST (see page 33).

DO then pay the debts with the highest rate of interest first – these are the ones that are costing you the most.

DO make sure that all your payments are set up to leave your account two days after you are paid – this way bills are paid before the money is spent on other things.

DON'T incur more debt to pay off debt (without seeking advice first).

DON'T necessarily pay the creditor who shouts the loudest – they are not always the ones who should take priority.

DON'T be tempted by the adverts for loans in the back of newspapers and on daytime television – the fees and charges for these loans can be sky-high and very often they will require your home as security for the loan.

Chapter 10

Last Resorts

Jack never would have thought that he would be joining the ever-increasing bankruptcy statistics. In fact, if someone had told him that the eventual outcome of his visit to me would be declaring himself bankrupt, he would not have come within a two-mile radius of our advice centre. But when he came to see me he was desperate. He was an older man and in debt as a result of signing guarantees so his son could borrow money to start a business. Sadly, due to some unwise business decisions taken by his son, the company folded and Jack lost all hope of his son paying him back. And that's when the phone calls from the various creditors began.

By the time Jack came to see me, matters had spiralled totally out of control. He was ashamed. He had always been so good with money and had just wanted to give his son a helping hand along the way. We worked through his income and expenditure and spoke at length about the different options open to him, but on his low income there was no way these debts would ever be repaid in his lifetime. And so we concluded together that bankruptcy would be the best solution for him. This was no snap decision. We had spent hours discussing the implications that bankruptcy would have for him and preparing him for the bankruptcy procedure.

If your debts are causing you immense pressure, you have explored the different options available to you and have concluded that there is no real prospect of your debts being repaid, then it may be that bankruptcy is the best option for you. OK, so now I've got a hunch that you're shouting at me: 'Me? Bankrupt? I don't think so!' But let me just remind you that our government has made legal provision for its citizens to opt for bankruptcy if appropriate. In other words, it's OK to go bankrupt; it is not a crime. What was once taboo is now an everyday occurrence and this is largely due to the government relaxing the rules on bankruptcy in recent years. But do hear me right. Bankruptcy is still, without question, *a last resort*. Anyone contemplating bankruptcy must fully explore the other options available to them before embarking on it.

Essentially, there are two ways of becoming bankrupt. First, any creditor to whom you owe at least £750 can apply to the court to make you bankrupt. (If one of your creditors applies to make you bankrupt, it's not too late to resolve this and you should seek advice straight away.) Secondly, you can apply for your own bankruptcy.

The effects of going bankrupt are the same whether you

make yourself bankrupt or whether someone to whom you owe money makes you bankrupt. Although bankruptcy has many restrictions and disadvantages, its main advantage is that once someone has been released from bankruptcy (usually after one year), all of their outstanding debts are written off and they can make a fresh start.

Bankruptcy usually lasts for a maximum of one year, after which the debtor becomes a 'discharged bankrupt', which basically means that they are not bankrupt any more. However, the black mark will remain and credit reference agencies will still hold details of the bankruptcy for six years. Someone in that situation would find it difficult to obtain credit during that time.

Whether bankruptcy is the right step will always depend on individual circumstances. If you are threatened with bankruptcy by one of your creditors or you are considering declaring yourself bankrupt you need to take advice on just how bankruptcy would affect you. At the end of the day, although bankruptcy can offer a fresh start to many who are struggling with the heavy burden of their debts, its implications are wide and its restrictions can be very limiting.

• If you are an owner-occupier you will nearly always lose your home.

• You risk losing your car, pension, savings and valuable assets.

• You may be required to hand over any income

which exceeds that which is necessary for you to live on.

• Your bank account could be affected and you are likely to be limited to a very basic account; that is, one with no overdraft.

• You will be unable to be a company director or hold any public office.

• You may be unable to continue to work in certain professional roles such as being a solicitor or accountant. If you are unsure, you should check with your governing body.

• You will be unable to obtain credit in excess of £500 without first disclosing your status as a bankrupt.

• You will have to pay a fee if you declare yourself bankrupt.

• If you are self-employed, you may have to cease trading.

• If it is felt that you have been dishonest or blameworthy, then you might have increased restrictions imposed on you. This is called a Bankruptcy Restriction Order and the bankruptcy will last longer than the usual one year.

However, in spite of all these negatives, for you, like Jack, it may still be the best option. This is something that a debt advisor would be able to explore fully with you. In my experience, for some people bankruptcy can be nothing short of a positive life-changing experience.

IVAs

An alternative to bankruptcy is an Individual Voluntary Arrangement (IVA). This is a legally binding agreement between yourself and your creditors. Typically, it involves making monthly payments for five years, at the end of which any outstanding debt is written off.

One of the main advantages of IVAs over bankruptcy is that you are more likely to be able to keep your home (although you may be required to release some of the equity – the difference between what you owe on the mortgage and what the house is worth). IVAs also bring restrictions, although these are less harsh than those imposed following bankruptcy.

If you are considering entering into an IVA, then first seek free legal advice from a debt counselling centre. There are companies that specialize in helping people achieve an IVA, but some of them make things worse, so be careful! IVAs can be very expensive and often require payment of hefty up-front fees. Also, if you breach the terms of the IVA agreement – that is – you don't keep up with the required payments, then your creditors can apply to make you bankrupt. IVAs are certainly not suitable for everyone and in fact the Consumer Credit Counselling Service (one of the leading debt advice agencies) only recommended IVAs to 3% of the people it advised in 2006.[24]

The Biggest Smile

Well, our time together is almost over, but just before we part I want to tell you about the biggest smile I have ever seen. When she came to see me four years ago Ruth was one of the saddest women I have ever met. Life had been hard for her. Her husband had walked out, leaving her with two small children and a drawer full of unopened demands from creditors. By this time, she was beside herself. She said, 'I had no idea we owed all this money. I don't even know what debts half the letters are talking about. I've just had a man on the phone chasing a catalogue debt who suggested I sell my wedding ring to send him some money.'

I made her a cup of tea, we got the two toddlers colouring and went through every letter, demand and the three court summonses she had. At the end of an hour she looked ashen. I said, 'It's going to be hard but we can get you through this.' She didn't look convinced, but she nodded.

Over the next few months and years that woman attacked her debts with a determination that was amazing.

I think at times she tried everything I have written about in this book apart from going bankrupt or getting an IVA. She budgeted, she wrote letters to creditors, she cut up her credit cards, we convinced a judge to let her spread the mortgage arrears over a long period and so keep her home, she not only tried 'Cash for a Month' – she *only* used cash! Whereas before her husband had handled all the finances, this woman now became an expert on the best phone deals and the cheapest insurance and changed her gas supplier three times! It's true that in the early days she was on the phone to me at least once a week, but I didn't mind. I soon came to realize that I was watching a pro!

I know it may sound trite but after a while I even came to believe she was enjoying it. One day I told her: 'You seem different – almost as if you are enjoying all this.' If she'd hit me I couldn't have complained, but she didn't. She just said, 'All my life people have told me that I'm useless with money: my father told me that, my friends told me and my husband used to scream it at me once a week. But now I know I'm not. It's true I've made lots of mistakes but that doesn't mean I've got to go on making them – and anyway most of my trouble came from that great financial guru that left me with all these debts. No Katie, you're not wrong – I am enjoying getting out of debt. For the first time in my life I'm in control.'

I suppose that conversation was about nine months after she first came to see me. But that wasn't when I saw the smile. No, a few years later was the last time she came to see me. It was in the school holidays and I was amazed at how much the kids had grown but more shocked by the transformation in their mum. It was like looking at a different woman. She said, 'Katie, I am debt free. Not the mortgage, of course, but all the rest – debt free!' She leant across the desk, kissed me, and then she smiled – the biggest, deepest, most wonderful smile I have ever seen.

I cried!

I want you to smile again too.

And you can.

I leave you with two one second pages. If you forget everything else, at least remember these!

If you spend more than you earn,
then sooner or later
you'll be broke.

... and the final One Second Page

If you consistently spend less than
you earn,
          then sooner or later
                    you'll be financially free.

The Future's Bright

I'm sure you've heard of that famous speech by Martin Luther King that begins, 'I have a dream...'. As we come to the end of our time together, I want to give you a dream. It's a few years down the road, you've worked hard at getting your debts under control, you've fought battles with your credit cards, you've scoured the Internet for the best deals – and at last even if you're not debt free, you've got control. But this is not just a dream. So many people I have advised over the years have achieved that reality – and you can too. But with that day in mind, here are ten golden rules to keep you on the straight and narrow.

• Regularly review your budget. Our finances are not set in stone and can often change for a whole number of reasons. Perhaps you have received a promotion, your lodger has moved out or your child has started college. Each of these will impact on what you can spend each month and may involve you carefully planning your spending to ensure the balance is not tipped in the wrong direction. This is why it's important to regularly get out your budget, dust it off, check whether it's still realistic and if necessary update it. This is also true if you decide you want to save for a holiday, a house move or a car – you may need to rework your budget to enable you to do this.

• Always try to spend a little (at least!) less than you earn. When calculating your budget, keep this golden rule in mind. Remember that most people spend about 10% more than they earn and that can only ever lead to debt in the long term.

• Set your own personal financial goals and keep these under review. An example might be that you decide to take an extended holiday in three years' time. You work out what the holiday will cost, including your spending money, and over the next few years you start to pay money into a savings account. How liberating to think that in three years you could be lying on a sun-kissed beach knowing that everything is paid for and you don't have to return home to face a scary credit card bill!

• Try saving a regular amount each month as a matter of habit. A recommended amount to save is 10% of your income. Just imagine: if you do this for ten years, you will have saved a whole year's income! By the way, it's no good waiting until the end of the month and then saving what money you've got left – the chances are it will be zero. I would suggest opening a separate savings account and setting up a monthly standing order to transfer money from your current account into the savings account soon after you've been paid. You will soon get used to living without this money and eventually won't even notice it's gone! All the while, a nice balance is accruing in your savings account.

• Try to build up an emergency fund equivalent to at least three months' salary. This is not for holidays or non-essential items. But it's there as a back-up or a buffer, giving you some security if you ever lost your job or fell ill. (I have known some free spirits who have used it to travel the world!)

• Check the rates of interest you are paying on any loans – including credit cards – and receiving on your accounts. Many people stay with the same mortgage provider for the whole length of their mortgage. But in this area there are normally no prizes for loyalty. It's the same with any loans and of course your precious savings as well. Always look around and choose accounts that have competitive rates of interest. And remember the power of compound interest! When you are borrowing, you're paying interest on interest and when you're debt free it works in your favour – you'll be earning interest on the interest you've already received. What could be better?

• Always read your statements and check your accounts carefully. So many people are falling victim to fraud (it happened to me twice in one month!). If you have any concerns, contact your bank straight away.

• During the course of the book, we've considered the importance of ensuring that you are getting the best value for money for your bills, utilities and mortgages. Keep this under constant review, as the offers are always changing as the different companies vie for customers. Keep reviewing the 'Save the Pennies', 'The Price is Right' and 'Dump the Debt' pages in this book. Sometimes the simple approaches make a massive difference.

• Make a point of regularly looking at websites such as www.moneysavingexpert.com and www. thisismoney.co.uk for ideas and information about how to make your money work best for you.

• Keep control! There are brilliant software options if you want to use your computer, for example Quicken or BankTree. Or, if you prefer, try a battered notebook. But however you do it, the goal is that from this day on there will be no surprises! You should know your current balance within a few pounds – at the very least, there should be no more panics at the cashpoint!

I hope you've enjoyed the book. Even more, I hope that you go for the dream of becoming free from the worry of financial pressure. But don't keep the good news to yourself – pass it on.

You're a debt buster!

References

1   Jane Baker, 'Are Holidays More Important Than Your Finances?', at www.fool.co.uk/news/your-money/2008/01/18/are-holidays-more-important-than-your-finances.aspx?source=iceinmeml0080001.

2   Martin Hickman, 'Banks Face Mass Legal Action over Loan Insurance Policies', at www.independent.co.uk/money/insurance/banks-face-mass-legal-action-over-loan-insurance-policies-822147.html.

3   'Turn Off the Light', www.biggreenswitch.co.uk/around_the_home/switch-lights-off.

4   www.biggreenswitch.co.uk/around_the_home/turn-down-thermostat.

5   Bill Wilson, 'Barclay Chief's Gaffe Recalls Ratner Howler', at http://news.bbc.co.uk/1/hi/business/3199822.stm.

6   www.creditaction.org.uk/assets/PDF/stats/2008/june.pdf.

7   www.news.bbc.co.uk, 13 December 2007.

8   Sarah Bell, 'Rise of the "White-Collar Tramp"', *Financial Mail on Sunday*, 14 December 2004.

9   This assumes that there is a monthly interest rate of 1.58%, that only 3% minimum is paid off, and that there are other debts on the card. Even after fifteen years, almost £1 out of the original £14.50 would still be outstanding.

10 www.fool.co.uk, 31 December 2007.

11 'Credit Card Repayment Calculator', www.moneyexpert.com/partners/aoluk/calc-pay-off-card.asp.

12 *Ibid.*

13 Niki Chesworth, 'Tips to Help Your Family Cope with Inflation', at www.telegraph.co.uk/money/main.jhtml?MLC=/money/personal_finance/pensions/article&xml=/money/2008/05/15/cminflation115.xml&CMP=ILC-mostviewedbox.

14 *Ibid.*

15 Jasmine Birtles and Jane Mack, *A Girl's Best Friend is Her Money*, London: Boxtree, 2002.

16 'Escape from Debt', Keith Tondeur, Credit Action, 1993.

17 'Drugs "Stop Compulsive Shopping"', at http://news.bbc.co.uk/1/hi/health/3077569.stm.

18 www.coastnews.com/health/affluenza/html, 14 July 2004.

19 www.hbo.com/city/episode/season4/episode64.shtml.

20 'Low-Energy Lightbulbs', at www.biggreenswitch.co.uk/energy_saving/low-energy-lightbulbs.

21 www.biggreenswitch.co.uk/around_the_home/standby-button.

22 'Mortgage Rescue Schemes', at http://england.shelter.org.uk/get_advice/advice_topics/paying_for_a_home/mortgage_arrears/mortgage_rescue_schemes.

23 www.creditaction.org.uk/assets/PDF/stats/2007/DebtStatisticsJune2007.pdf.

24 http://www.moneysavingexpert.com/loans/pdf-iva-guide.pdf

Appendix

INCOME	
Type	**£ per week or month**
Basic salary/wages	
Partner's basic salary/wages	
Guaranteed overtime	
Partner's guaranteed overtime	
Bonuses	
Partner's bonuses	
Pension	
Child benefit	
Income support	
Jobseeker's Allowance	
Tax credits	
Maintenance/child support	
Other benefits (1)	
(2)	
Other income (1)	
(2)	
Total	

EXPENDITURE	
	Weekly/monthly £
Mortgage/rent	
Second mortgage	
Endowment	
Ground rent	
Building insurance	
Contents insurance	
Council tax	
Water rates	
Gas	
Electricity	
Coal/oil	
Telephone/mobile phone	
TV licence/TV subscriptions	
TV rental	
Fines	
Petrol	
Car tax	
Car insurance	
Car servicing/repairs	
Car loan	
Pension	
Life insurance	
Child care	
Maintenance	

EXPENDITURE (cont'd)	
	Weekly/monthly £
House repairs/decoration	
Charitable giving	
Regular savings	
Housekeeping (food and cleaning supplies)	
Prescriptions	
Launderette/dry cleaning	
Newspapers	
Cigarettes	
Clothes	
Hobbies/sports/toys	
Entertainment	
Meals out/takeaways	
Gambling/bingo	
Christmas/birthday presents	
Holidays	
Emergencies	
Travel to work/school	
School dinners/meals at work	
Other school expenses	
Pocket money	
Pets	
Other (1)	
(2)	
Total	

Debt	Amount owed	Interest rate (%)
Gas		
Electricity		
Mortgage		
Council Tax		
Hire purchase on car		
Bank overdraft		
Bank loan		
Credit card 1		
Credit card 2		
Credit card 3		
Store card		
Catalogue purchases		
TOTAL	£	

Useful Contacts

Citizens Advice Bureaux
Tel: see your local telephone directory
www.adviceguide.org.uk

Consumer Credit Counselling Service (CCCS)
Wade House, Merrion Centre, Leeds, LS2 8NG
Tel: 0800 138 1111
www.cccs.co.uk

Credit Action
2 Ridgmount Street, London, WC1E 7AA
Tel: 0207 436 9937
www.creditaction.org.uk

National Debtline
Tricorn House, 51–53 Hagley Road, Edgbaston, Birmingham, B16 8TP
Tel: 0808 808 4000
www.nationaldebtline.co.uk

Christians Against Poverty
(They work with people of all faiths or no faith)
Jubilee Mill, North Street, Bradford, BD1 4EW
Tel: 01274 760720
www.capuk.org